Finding that Warmth in the Frosty Nights

Finding that Warmth in the Frosty Nights

Roshana Nazari Kirchhofer

To order additional copies of this book, contact:
Xlibris
1-888-795-4274
www.Xlibris.com
Orders@Xlibris.com
793768

Contents

The Essence

The time spent with you is full of pleasure.
I can't even measure.
I never want a closure.
It's willingly and not a pressure.
It's euphoric and a treasure.
In every mirror, you are amazing and a great refresher
And a deep, dark, unseen cave adventure,
Which is always raising my natural dopamine and arterial blood pressure.

Pairs

Why don't you see the intense blinding light in the dark?
Why can't you feel the calm blue ocean in the hot blazing desert?
Why wouldn't you find sweetness in the intense bitter drink?
Everything exists in pairs, so choose the sweet one.

Anxiety

Alcohol helps it better than sobriety.
That is not a good option, though; heal yourself with
self-therapy and quietly.
It's a common issue in our society,
And unfortunately it's not easy to deal with or there
are therapy of variety.
Yes, it takes a long time to gain control of the anxious
emotions and to recover,
But it is not impossible for the cause to be discovered.
I am speaking from personal experience that took me
five years plus to heal and uncover.
No one can help effectively other than yourself, with
your innate will power from such a drag and suffer.
I am trying to help and be your buffer. You can
initiate now, and you will be better by the summer
and thereafter.
Once you are able to conquer the draining disturbance
of anxiety, then inner peace and harmony is going be
your
Permanent lover.

Juliet without Romeo

The battle was not with you and I
But with me, my, and I.
The passion, love, and devotion within me won the
war with hate for you.
It got clear that you are not my Romeo,
But I am your die-hard and bleeding Juliet.

His First Birthday

My sleep is low,
But you make my heart glow.
I bought you your favorite birthday toy.
You have brought my heart so much joy.
You have grown and learned so much in just one year,
And let me enlighten that has just left me
mesmerized, thrilled, and with a one-derful year.
Oh, my son and my dear,
I love you as deep as ocean floor, and
you are my forever amour.

Friends . . .

I love rhyming,
Even better with great company and dining.
I get my aspiration from my great friends who are
just sparkling.
I can't even help it, the words are just fluent and
lining
And making both of us just have long miles of smiling!

Unforgettable Sounds

Your voice,
It's the most deep, sensual, with perfect speed and
balanced sounds I have ever heard from any human
being.
Doesn't matter the content of what you deliver, as long
as you make a noise,
It makes my walls melt and potentially make a lethal
choice.
Your voice is so delicate, so I offer you a sweet drink
for your tongue to be kept moist.
You even make profanity sound delightful and
rejoiced.
Oh, so don't stop talking, let everyone hear your radio
voice.

Improve History

Why do blacks and whites still fight?
They should complement each other like salt and
pepper and act peacefully and tight.
Turn off that hating light, and make our society
loving and inspiring field and sight.

Got to Love Our Man

When she speaks, she is known as a comedian.
When she writes, she is labeled as a poet.
When she works, she is called a nurse.
When she cares, she is a mother.
When she gets dolled up for social gatherings, she is
known as a sister and a friend,
But when she is compelled to be mad and yell, she is
known as a wife.
She is no perfect human and always desires to enhance
her life
And always is climbing the high mountains and all
about that strive.

The Hurricane

Often I see one line of words, but then I read several
translations of that same word or line.
I cannot shut down my brain.
I want to cut that train
That's causing me a whole lot of strain.
I want my sanity to maintain.
I don't want to complain again and again.
Yes, I agree, it is exercising my brain,
But sometimes I just want to shut down the hurricane
And then enjoy and have a sweet pink and carbonated
champagne.

She, The Titanium

You left her
Like a fish outside of the water.
You are back and expect her to be alive, stronger and
taller.
And NOW you are ready to adore her?
Hmm . . . she is titanium, at last, and will not open
her welcoming arms because you well taught
Her.

Be Polite, She Will Treat You with Light

Use your mother's taught wisdom and don't call any woman:
Fat, pregnant, old, or even angry. Because even if we are, we really are not!

Quality Time

Take me to fine dining
With superior quality, wining
Under the moonlighting,
And then go to the beach, hear the wave crashing,
Do soul searching, and finding
Enough of this rhyming.
Dreaming big, anytime is the perfect timing.

Appreciate Alive

Alive people appreciates flowers
And not when we shower their graves with sunflowers.
Chest risings are able to see, feel, and smell the love.
Underground bodies do not even care about blown-
away flowers
with strong and loud wind powers.

Middle Child

*She is one of the five children of the family.
And she is the chosen one
to not be the chosen one
but the forgotten one.*

Extroverted Externally and Introverted Internally

Excuse me for being an extrovert.
Nothing has changed ever since my birth.
It's a positive attribute, they say, because it keeps the
people in my presence awake (for my shocking/radical
comments) and alert.
Oh, I am also informed that I am a delight, polite,
sweet, and soft like a crème brûlée dessert.

Prescription: Laughter 100 milligrams PO PRN Daily

They call me a laugh doctor.
I prescribe a dose of laughter,
Which increases the heart rate, and then I administer the IV beta blocker,
Which ends the story with labeta-LOL (name of the fast heart rate medication),
so it still is about a dose of laugggghter.

No More Lemonade!

Life has given me the lemon.
Instead of lemonade,
I have made the lemon capers chicken
Because protein is better than the sweet and silent
enemy: sugar in our kitchen.

Dripping Rain

I want to cry.
That's how sometimes I get by.
I am by myself, me and I.
Crying unloads and makes me ready to once again fly.
I cry in the dark and smile in the light,
But the smile is no lie.
Crying is not only for one occasion, but also for many
reasons like the many different flavor pieces of a pie:
Sadness, excitement, and tears of joy.
This life is dynamic,
cycle of life is full of life, and then you die.
Sometimes you say "hi," and other times you have to
express your deepest goodbye.

Ideal Bond

Relationships are not driven by force or friction.
It has to be real and nonfiction.
With reasonable amount of time, it should feel
unguarded, affectionate, passionate, and natural
euphoric addictions.
It has to be mutual like each other's reflections.

Emotional Abuse

It leaves her with nothing but the blues.
It suffocates her with emotional scars and deep bruise.
She is often misunderstood, wronged, and accused.
It is above challenging at times for her to feel and act
motivated and enthused.
She senses like she wants to be alone or take off for a
long silent and peaceful cruise
Or even take a prolonged snooze.

Bright Side

Roses are not roses without thorns.
Pleasure doesn't come without moans.
Unicorns don't exist with three horns.
Sun always shines after gloomy and loud storms

Heart to Heart

Eye contact gives the heart imagination.
It's enriched with deep information.
It makes no mistake nor accusation.
It is nonverbal of the heart-to-heart exchange of
sensation.
It elevates heart rate, blood pressure, natural
endorphins, and calls for a celebration.

Romance

Your love shelters me like a natural protected cove.
It feels as pure as a baby dove.
You treat me as your priority of all the above.
Once you got to know me, then you took a head dove.
That is why I can trust you, and you are someone I can never get bored or tired of.

Mother

Oh, my mother,
You are so kind, loving, supportive, and unbreakable
like a leather
But also soft, gentle, caring, and beautiful like a pure
dove feather.
Your love is always displayed with warmth, no matter
what, like a sauna temperature.
Even though your mood swings are like extreme
seasons as tornado weather,
You still cherish us like there is no other.
Most essentially, you keep the family bond strong and
all of us together.
So as we get older, we enormously appreciate you, our
beloved mother.

Uncherished Heart

My heart and soul have been damaged,
and they can't be fixed with a simple thin bandage.
I have given you the message,
So sprint, having this knowledge.
I am not your average damaged but deep and long
mileage.
Thus, I want to be alone romantically because that's
the state I am comfortable in,
and I don't want my heart to have any more of the
hemorrhage.
And this is the truth about my uncherished heart's life
leakage, and all the pieces are carnage.

I Love My Boy

He is my bundle of troubles but a joy.
He loves to play all day with his Thomas the Trains
and still asks me to buy him more train toys.
He spends quality time with Mommy, whether in
cooking, reading, building, or with Dada in the
garage; he just enjoys.
He makes smart and age-appropriate choices,
And he surely doesn't like timeouts and being in
trouble,
So he tries hard and collectively avoids it.
But what can you do? Boys are just going to be active
boys.

Hazardous Habit

Fellows, please stop smoking
Because later in life, your lungs are going to feel like
failing and that you are choking.
With chronic obstructive pulmonary disease, you're
going to have low oxygen and carbo loading,
As it will not be thrilling or chilling with your coping,
So stop smoking and let the beautiful natural oxygen/
gas exchange occurring, circulating, and
Floooowing!

Painless Love

You made it easy to make me your lover.
I am so deep into you that it's too late to recover.
There are abundant of traits about each other yet to
discover.
Love me endlessly, like there is no other.
When I don't see or talk to you, it's a bummer.
It warms my heart to know that you are so
understanding and a giver.
Considering all, it makes it natural and
uncomplicated to be your lover!

Introducing to Santa Clause

Don't cry, my apple pie.
You are so cool and fly.
You will fly super high, my butterfly.
And so always try your best and don't be shy.
My love for you is always multiplied and magnified.
Santa Claus is nice, so don't be terrified.
Have fun with Santa by asking what you want for Christmas.
And the memories you have created with each Santa picture are beautified and amplified.

Tranquility

Sleep peacefully, my child, with no fear
when Mommy is here.
I will stay by you and sing to you softly just as you're
near.
Take your time to fall asleep, my dear.
But don't take forever as Mommy is running out of
words
Because Momma isn't Dr. Seuss or Shakespeare.

The Breakup

I am detached before I get my heart more scratched
As our feelings are not mutual.
We are not compatible and are rather a mismatch.
So it's better to detach now prior to us having a heated
boxing match.

Silently Exploring

You are so near but feels very far.
We should go out in one or two bars,
But be careful not to hit my leg to prevent a war.
I wish I was not at work and was soaring in the sky and touching stars
And pleasing them to heal my scars.
Enough of this, I want to go find a salad bar
While you play your steel guitar and smoke a cigar,
And we feel like rock stars.

Active Boy

I love my brave Tyler.
He roars like a tiger.
I cannot wait for him to be able to get vocal and go
exhilarating places with me, I am so eager.
We would go bowling because he is a star striker.
He will ask to go for a hike, though, as he is a fast
hiker,
But we cannot because outdoors, the weather is 3
degrees Fahrenheit freezer.

Attaining Education

One immense part of life is learning and school.
It practices your brain hemispheres and provides your
soul with fuel,
And it also offers you with some vast life tools.
With all the acquired wisdom and knowledge you will
gain,
All the girls will be after you and drool.
You have an enormous potential, and remember, no
one is ever too cool for school.

Mother's Goal

You are my sweetness,
Also uniqueness.
Hopefully, I will be an ideal mother and make you feel
independent, safe, secure, and complete.
You are intelligent and will figure out life and its
neatness.
You are going to have tremendous amount of
strengths and just a few weaknesses.
You are so energetic, and I appreciate your kind and
warm-heartedness.

The Divine Power

We love God.
He is more important than the iPod.
So obey his life rules and try your hardest, even if you
think you cannot.
I am not demanding to be a robot,
But respect, obey, listen, and love him a lot.
And for that, he will make your life as sweet as an
apricot.

The Sound Guardians

Listen and follow the advice and guidance of your
parents.
They are the ones who have your clearance.
Also, if you want nice presents, then you better listen
to your parents,
Not just now but also later in life for your
inheritance.
You are dependent until eighteen years of age.
Then you will graduate with your conquered, fully
and legally independence.

Exertion

One of the greatest teachers of life is pain.
Without pain, there is little deep involvement of the
brain and no gain.
Pain makes you think, learn, reflect, and explain;
Makes your train of thoughts deep and long like a
certain transporting train.
So just know pain is part of life growth,
So it's essential to experience and attain.
It's not there to be vain or go to the subconscious mind,
also known as down the drain.
Learn to stay strong, cope, and do not strain others by
your constant complaints.

Rejections Are Okay

You asked for your space,
So you are getting what you wished for because I am
independent and not a nut case.
My heart's window is closed and has no more
available space or place.
This is not an assumption, but on a given verbal
knowledge base,
I am not continuing involvement with someone who
does not want to be chased,
As this is supposed to be an adult relationship and not
a game or a race.

The Holiday Spirits

I love the holidays and the Christmas tree.
Even while I am traveling, I close my eyes, and feeling
the spirit is the key.
I will get to see a white winter this year and cannot
wait to do my favorite winter sport, skiing.
Anyways, enjoy your evening with some full of
antioxidant green cup of tea.

Artistic Liar

You are a beautiful and innovative liar.
I cannot believe you even if you say it higher and
higher.
You may have the heat of the moment's desire,
But lying is not required.
The truth has transpired.
Liars are not so much desired or admired.

Eldest Sister!

༄

You are an amazing sister.
You were always present for all of us, regardless, even
if you had bloody and un-healing blisters.
I am sure our dad is watching from heaven and is a
proud mister.
Happy birthday, my dear sister!

ൕ

Second Eldest Sister

Roy, you are a sister full of joy!
What would you like as your birthday gift or toy?
Hope that what I got for you, you will enjoy!
Happy birthday, my dear Roy.

Play-Name
Doddle

I see you as a jewel.
Do not be cruel and brutal.
If you do not understand women, search it up well in
the Google,
And please stop petting every other poodle!

Nurses!

I like to make people laugh.
It's bearable than infection staph.
Nurses are working on vital signs graph,
While respiratory therapists are giving a breathing
treatment or a puff.
Some people are at lunch, finally, and simply eating
half of the calf.
Now, everyone, gather, pretend you love each other,
for the ER yearbook photograph.

Numbness

My heart feels Kentucky-weather cold.
Being romantically alone is bold and gold.
It does not want to be held.
Nothing is told that can be sold.
It's my ocean-deep sound decision,
So I do not want to be reprimanded or scolded.
I just want to be here alone in my household,
Relax, be at peace, and unfold,
And tell stories that are untold.

The Toddler Phase

My son Tyler,
You are such a smiler
And have a fine taste in clothes and is a great styler,
Wants to inquire different toys and so are a big baller
and buyer.
You act so independent from day one, but remember,
you are still a two-year-old minor.
You are full of energy, active, and a little hyper.
Your personality is flames and fire,
And you execute yourself as a tiger.
Oh, my Tyler!

Hiking Days

At the blue and beautiful Laguna Beach,
After three hours of hiking, we finally reached.
Doing a little picnic now and flavoring some sweet peach.
Hope you all are having a bright day as well.
Now I am done delivering my speech.

A Rich Oxygen Environment/Hobby

I love to hike.
There is nothing else that is as comparable that I like.
I want to push myself today to the next level of
mountain bike.
But first, I need to get Starbucks coffee known as the
dark pike.

Proving Others Wrong

They say you are what you eat.
I ate sushi today,
So that makes me a mermaid,
And so not sure how I will drive home.
Flying is the only option; here I am, ready now to
roam!

Admiring the Clear Sky

Do you want to lie horizontally in a hammock and
watch the clear sky full of twinkling stars?
Be careful, don't fall in the semi-darkness and sustain
bad scars.
Please bring your instrument outside, add to the
mood, and play your favorite song with your guitar.

As If a Candle

If you do not ignite me,
I cannot provide you with scent or light.
I do not ask for the ignition or care to engage in a
fight.
If you want the light, then you take the initiative all
on your own will and delight.
And if you do not feel like it, then it's just quite all
right.
Not everyone has a mature and wise appetite.
Now have a good and tight night!
And have a vivid memory and sight!

Insomniacs

It is 2:00 a.m., and so please try to fall sleep,
Not just non-rapid eye movement, lightly,
But get the rapid eye movement cycle and deep.
Otherwise, later at work, you will feel exhausted,
irritated, unfocused, and want to loudly weep.
Turn off your cellphone to stop social media
notification sounds, ding-ding or beep-beep,
And gain few more hours of beauty and much-needed
sleep.

ß

Negative Voice

Your life struggles, the negative voices, and your
resident inner demons,
Everyone possesses them, does not matter your ethnic
background or your geographical regions.
It wants to leave you with heartaches, sadness,
depression, and long-lasting lesions,
Not just one occasion but also all seasons.
But fight it and fight it immensely with all of your
warm, radiating powerful senses and your
Universal religions.
Stand strong against it with your profound mighty
positions
And enlighten it that you are on an impermeable and
indestructible mission.
You will not allow the demons for your deletion or
depletion!

Favorite Day of the Week!

Today is Friday.
Everyone is happy and not spicy or feisty.
It's going to be an appeasing and eventful nighty.
It is going to be profound nightlife that is shiny and not tiny.
Thus, we're going to live it up fully, brightly, and nicely!

Week Ended

Everyone looks forward to the decompression time or
the weekend.
For the labor force, it is the happiest time of the week
and the highest end.
We are so lucky that the weekend is the mandatory
labor law and really godsend,
So we do not have to get shut down if our weak voice
recommend.
We have no bosses to obey, please, or pretend.
We all wish that we could have our weekends forever
extend.
But for now, we can sit back, comfortable in our
breathable cotton pajamas, eating pizza and
Feeling all content.
And this is the serenity, the weekend.

The Energy Source

I love cooking.
Everybody eats it so fast as if it is as sweet as vanilla
pudding.
I mix all the spices in such a manner that they are in
a great marriage and are not arguing or fighting.
It leaves the audience asking for more, like Beyoncé's
love songs, and bowl-licking.
Food is an essential part of the body and soul for every
human ethnicity.
If one cannot cook, it's okay, do not panic, just use
YouTube recipes and logic.
Now please savor a flavorful scenic picnic.

The Zoo

Weather is great tomorrow, so I am taking my tiger
Tyler to the zoo.
Who would like to take their little cubs too
Where they are going to learn more about animals
and have fun too?
I like to expose him to unique experiences and
opportunities more than just a few,
And it will make your bond with them stronger like a
super glue.
We will explore some then take a break and have a
bite to chew,
And hopefully, their menu has the delicious beef stew
with cashew.
I think tomorrow will be one exciting day that I will
accrue with my boo.

The Tale of Life

It has moments of feeling blue and low,
but it also has splits of high spirits and high fives.
It can be unpredictable, negative, and
counterintuitive,
And sometimes it makes you want to be out on the
stage for a loud and proud, skilled
Performance, and other times it makes you want to
hide and be a fugitive.
Accept and cherish all the colors and discolorations of
life lessons because constant effortless
and unchallenged life is not realistic or durative.
Be the driver of your own life and be creative and
curative.
It's you and only you who can be your own life's
compliment and make it decorative.
Take your chances, strive for the highest and your best
potential.
Thus, be the universe's or life's positive representative!

Intuition/The Sixth Sense

Life experiences are essential and requisition.
With life burns, you learn to believe your intuition.
It is built in us to protect us and guide our decision.
It is not meant for our division.

Beauty in Any Weight

You are always skinny with any weight.
Why are you so worried about your size, my friend?
You are skinny in any state.
If you need encouragement to stay fit, I do not mind
pushing you. That is great.
So here we go.
Please stop becoming one with sweets, carbs, delicious,
and rich Pakistani food too.
The food portion consumption is the key, so lessen the
chew.
It's easier said than done.
Only some individuals have the discipline and the
mind power to lose and maintain,
So prove that you are one of the few.
If one day is not effective, not an issue, wake up the
next day and redo.

The Love Games

❧

Why do people play games in the relationships,
Ideally and supposed to be loving, giving,
compassionate, tolerant, and a partnership?
If it feels real and deep, then one continues; if not, then
they shouldn't because that's when one
Starts the mind and behavior games,
And that initiates the disagreements, emotional
agony, permanent damage, and battleship.
Real love experience feels in the core and makes you
think and feel like you are soaring and floating high
in the spaceship.
Love heals, comforts, and secures the heart and
the soul because of the genuine compromise and
passionate companionship.

☙

The Essence of Life: Humble

Be humble
Because with any given era, anyone can lose it all
with a simple life tumble.
Nothing in life is a guaranteed but a gamble.
It's better to master early than in the highest peak of
the scramble.

Leaving Hospital against Medical Advice

When you go to the ER, expect a poke with a needle.
A doctor cannot diagnose until blood tests, radiology studies are performed, for real.
There are no magic healing prayer or fuel to fill you like a diesel.
This is modern medicine and not of medieval times.
So if you do not cooperate, then you are a free bird to fly home and label yourself as self-induced destructive individual
And hope and pray that you do not have to arrange your own funeral.

Effects of Love

Your love heals me.
Your attention glows me.
Your kindness repairs me.
Your giving steals me.
Your understanding cheers me.
Your passion kneels me.
Your tolerance blooms me.
Your action brightens me,
And my unconditional love for you feels me.

Women: Fire or Water

Furious women are like fire.
There are not a lot that they expect or require.
There are no other creations that are able to endorse
love like them,
But they have the basic love needs and a few things
they absolutely require.
If you fulfill their needs, then women are like water
and will wear your provided any color attire.

Actions Are Louder Than Words

Your voice talks to my ears,
But your actions speak directly to my heart and soul
and brings me to long pouring tears.
Your words say you care,
But your actions illustrate a clear picture of me being
your burden and despair.
Realizing that I cannot even breathe air
Makes me feel like a delicate piece of silk cloth that is
sheared and torn,
And I wonder if we'll ever get repaired.
I understand that a lot of work is required,
And I am here with my open heart and soul, ready for
anything and prepared.
And I am brave and not scared,
But you have to be willing to fix us, the pair that is
impaired.

The Time

How could you be so warm, loving, and caring to
form a bond
Then to just turn around and act freezing cold like a
snow in the wintertime?
You have broken an unguarded loving heart and
committed a love crime.
I miss the closeness, the bond, and crave back my
yesterday's sunshine.
If you do not feel the same anymore, that is completely
understandable and fine,
But at least explain your view and define.
I just cannot comprehend or digest your extremes.
So please provide me with the answer pill or enzyme.
My instinct has always been my vivid guide,
which I ignored that it has always been your
theatrical play and games.
The time and distance has been my coach.
Your departure has left me with sour taste in my soul
like a rotten lime.
I know this experience is supposed to teach me a life
lesson or even write a song and rhyme.
Sorry to say what goes round comes around.
It is just a matter of time.

Positivity: The Leader and the Winner

Sweetness in bitter days,
Positivity in the deeply negative days,
Good on evil days,
Sharpness in the intense dull days,
Happiness in the soul-damaging sad days,
Light in the dark days,
Activity in the lazy days;
It's all about how your perspective and feeling drives
And plays in so many different ways,
So train your brain to always be positive and shine in
every life lessons and phase!

Don't Manipulate

I got a full pouring plate.
I will choose not to participate
because there is no point.
It only stimulates the agony, frustration, and do us
apart.
I wore it in my body and soul for ten years,
Can't endure anymore,
So screaming sorry won't be effective.
It's a little too late.
Beneficial for you will be mental therapy and
rehabilitate.

Conserve Your Words

Conserve your thoughts.
Conserve your assets for someone who will love you for your worth.
Conserve it for the imperfectly perfect who sees you as not a short buy but a gently growing investment port.

He Dropped Me Like a Bungee Jump

He cut the rob as fast as he could
to free me from the pain and free drop
or really throw me out of his band.
Why couldn't you verbalize it to me like a brave-
hearted man?
Now that you have left, my peaceful sleep has begun.
You shouldn't have lied just for the sake of your
return.
I would have taken the truth rather because I am not
a gibberish fan.

You Can Be a Player

You can be a player,
but I don't have to be a gamer.
You can play solo or find a compatible player.
I am out, and I feel at ease but a stubborn winner.
You are not the loser, I just decided to peace out
earlier than later.

The Core Element of Life: Water

*It is neutral and is a life feeder
But can drop the pH and transform into acid and
burn her
but not save her.
So choose to be selective of the friends you
surround her.*

Soul and Superficial Flesh

Not connected at a younger in us
But a later in life of us.
Search it. It's shy, takes time like a crossing long road
snail,
but eventually, it's not dry and pale.

Practical Love

I love the way you love me.
I love the hour you love me.
I love the stress you deplete within me.
I love the heavy mountain you carry for me.
I love the care you show me.
I don't even speak a word,
But you already heard me,
And I entirely mutilated your Ferrari.
Do you still love me?

Toxicity

You make suffering look appealing and appeasing,
Though I have no desire to be repeating and reliving.

Evening Reflection

Staring at the angry deep-orange sun and blue sky,
It makes my soul crunch and cry,
Leaves my eyes dry.
There are no more tears left to shed
Because all the hatred, suffering, greed, cruelty,
corruption, and poverty numb the emotions and left
Mother Earth to fry and die.
We are getting ready to soon express our wretched
goodbye.

Siberian-Hearted

You left me dead.
Death found me and kissed me back to life, smoother
than you ever did try.

Matter . . .

Too enticing is material,
But it will not accompany anyone in their burial.
Constructing interior is richer than exterior.
Mastering it feels at peace, rich and superior.

A Child's Love Equation

The inner child's voice echoed,
Pain only knows how to deliver pain,
But make pain hand love.
Love is the main gain.
Then the cycle shall repeat and retain . . .

Power Is Beauty

Be the flower.
It signifies no weakness but power.
Hold your chin and standards as high as Eiffel Tower.
Your charisma is saturated with power.
Every day spent with you counts as a happy hour,
And please demonstrate to us again the red rose petal
shower.

Graceful Confidence

I don't take the passive way
If my heart feels it is my turn to stand for the battle.
I am not subjectively right,
but the universe is by my side.
I respect and don't belittle the opponent.
This is the resilient me, an active warrior and not a
no-action worrier.
I win the wars,
Not with my swords,
but with the colorful art of words, and then I find me
calm and settled.

Past Is Only a Lesson

I forgive you
For inflicting on me so much torment and pain.
The pain has loved me more than your offer could
ever extend.
Throb is what held me tight with its full intensity and
squeezed my heart.
Pain is more merciful than your excruciating and
precise dart.
The light shines even brighter and warmer now in my
center like the sun's reflection in the mirror.
Do you ever reflect on your error?
It's okay, I see it more clearly.
I found happiness, and you are no more of my shearer.

Their Purpose

No motivation to disclose of how you made me feel.
It does not faze you, it's no big deal.
Your true colors have surfaced and have been
revealed.
You only wanted to steal
And never ever intended to kneel.

Limitless Ocean

No one holds and executes love like a passionate
woman.
She has a lot to offer and deliver,
Loaded with aroma and therapeutic actions.
No need to preach her of love,
She is gorgeously natural and automatic.
Her touch is magnetic.
Her love is energetic, electric, and magic.

More Produces More

&

If you proceed cold,
I am freezing.
If you proceed warm,
I am boiling in oil and fever.

&

Pure Reached
the Damaged

Not every arrow aimed at my heart matched the
target.
Then you came to sight,
Melted my walls and enthused me to wave goodbye to
being guarded,
And seasoned my center with open warmth and
wholehearted.

Hope . . .

You drowned me in the ocean of your love,
Also rescued me to fly like a free-flying dove.
What are your intentions?
Your mysterious self intrigues me on what is your
next move.
Provide me protection with more than just a glove.

Pick Wisely

Life with love flourishes the heart,
Life with love drains the heart;
Depends on the delivery man.

Young Dating

The sparking smiles for miles
When I come to your sight,
I could sense your invasiveness to have us pile.
Why wait?
I already have been waiting for a while.
I am not hinting for us to legally file
But suggesting having a trial for just a mile.

Desirable Poison

Until death do us part.
You killed the soul of my soul,
Dissected me apart, and deported the devotion and
art of heart.
You make any of the past agony small and pain
pleasurable.
I bear the torture and stand strongly tall
With an untouchable dense wall.

The Influencer

The leader, the sun,
The only star that holds all the planets in their orbits
with its gravitational force like the words in a song,
Life depends on its powerful energy, light, and heat for
very long;
Influences our strength with vitamin D and human
life has been prolonged.
Highest positive energy of the universe, nothing but
the sun.
So be the sun that you already are and impact the
universe like the king of the world,
And the audience can join you or just watch you
radiate radiant heat and twirl.

CPSIA information can be obtained
at www.ICGtesting.com
Printed in the USA
LVHW112257280620
659239LV00001B/20